DISCOVERING GERMAN FOOTBALL

2020/21 SEASON

JOHN ALDER

CONTENTS

Introduction vii

1. PLANNING YOUR TRIP 1
   Deciding where to go 1
   Berlin 2
   Düsseldorf 2
   Frankfurt 2
   Hamburg 3
   Hannover 3
   Leipzig 3
   Munich 3
   Stuttgart 4
   Choosing clubs and games 4
   'Matchday' means 'match weekend' 5
   Look out for English weeks 5
   Getting a ticket 6
   Should I stand or sit? 6

2. GETTING THERE 8
   Types of train 8
   Long distance 8
   Regional 9
   Local 9
   Saving money 9
   Long distance buses 10
   Local travel 10
   Look out for free matchday travel 11
   Other helpful travel websites 11

3. THE TOP THREE DIVISIONS AT A GLANCE 13
   Die Bundesliga 13
   Die 2. Bundesliga 26
   Die 3. Liga 39

4. German for the football fan	54
5. WHO GOES UP AND WHO GOES DOWN?	59
Bundesliga	59
2. Bundesliga	60
3. Liga	61
Regionalligen	62
Oberligen	62
Level 6 and below	62
6. CUP COMPETITIONS	63
DFB-Pokal	63
DFL-Supercup	65
Verbandspokale	65
7. Finding out more	66
8. MAKING THE MOST OF YOUR VISIT	75
Come for a long weekend	75
Berlin	76
Düsseldorf	79
Frankfurt	84
Hamburg	86
Hannover	88
Leipzig	90
Munich	93
Stuttgart	95
9. Final words	98
Also by John Alder	99

Copyright © 2018 by John Alder

All rights reserved.

No part of this book may be reproduced in any form or by any electronic or mechanical means, including information storage and retrieval systems, without written permission from the author, except for the use of brief quotations in a book review.

❦ Created with Vellum

INTRODUCTION

- Are you a football fan who wants to see top quality football played with skill, passion and commitment in front of capacity crowds in some of the best stadiums in the world?
- Do you want to experience the nerve-tingling atmosphere of a German football match?
- Do you want to join fans who are proud of their roots and traditions and who care deeply about their football?
- Are you an independent-minded traveller who wants more than the sanitised and sentimentalised experience provided by mass tourism?
- Do you want to follow German football from home?

If your answer to any of these questions is "Yes'," then this book is meant for you.

It is for anyone who is thinking about going to watch a match, or who wants to find out more about the game in Germany.

Planning your trip covers practical things like deciding where and when to go, how to buy tickets.

In *Getting There*, you will learn about the best ways to travel to and in Germany.

The clubs of the top three divisions provides the critical information and links you will need to buy your tickets, find out about the clubs and get to the games.

German for the football fan will help you understand a bit of what is going on inside the ground

Who goes up and down? explains how the leagues work.

Cup Competitions describes the cups German clubs compete for.

Finding out more shows you the best ways to follow German football from home. It presents my favourite German football books as well as the websites and blogs I find most useful.

Making the most of your visit identifies cities you might use as a base for a football trip and things to do before and after the game.

1

PLANNING YOUR TRIP

Deciding where to go

Borussia Dortmund and Bayern Munich are the best-known clubs in Germany, but it can be difficult and expensive to get hold of tickets. The experience of watching less famous teams can be just as exciting.

And you don't have to restrict yourself to Bundesliga clubs. You will enjoy fantastic days out at 2. Bundesliga and 3. Liga grounds.

You will get the widest choice if you base yourself at a city with good transport links and that is within a cluster of clubs. For example, Leipzig has an airport with flights to and from six UK cities. It is home to a Bundesliga club (RB Leipzig) and is within easy reach of two second division and five third division teams.

Here is a list of possible bases and the clubs you could visit.

Berlin

You can fly there from Bristol, Manchester, East Midlands, Edinburgh, Glasgow, Liverpool, Gatwick, Heathrow, Luton, Southend, Stansted.

You can easily get to Hertha Berlin, RB Leipzig, 1 FC Union Berlin, SG Dynamo Dresden, 1 FC Magdeburg, Hallescher FC, Energie Cottbus.

Düsseldorf

You can fly there from Birmingham, Cardiff, Glasgow, Leeds, London City, Gatwick, Heathrow, Stansted, Manchester, Newcastle, Newquay.

You can easily get to Borussia Dortmund, Schalke 04, Bayer 04 Leverkusen, VfL Borussia Mönchengladbach, 1 FC Köln, VfL Bochum, Fortuna Düsseldorf, MSV Duisburg, SC Fortuna Köln, SC Preußen Münster, VfL Osnabrück, SV Meppen.

Frankfurt

You can fly there from Aberdeen, Birmingham, Bristol, Edinburgh, Glasgow, London City, Heathrow, Manchester, Newcastle.

You can easily get to Eintracht Frankfurt, 1 FSV Mainz, SC Darmstadt, 1 FC Kaiserslautern, Würzburger Kickers, Wehen Wiesbaden, FSV Frankfurt.

Hamburg

You can fly there from Aberdeen, Birmingham, Bristol, Edinburgh, Glasgow, London City, Gatwick, Heathrow, Luton, Manchester, Stansted.

You can easily get to Hamburger SV, SV Werder Bremen, FC St Pauli, FC Hansa Rostock, Holstein Kiel.

Hannover

You can fly there from Aberdeen, Edinburgh, Heathrow, Manchester, Stansted.

You can easily get to Hannover 96, VfL Wolfsburg, Eintracht Braunschweig, Armenia Bielefeld, SC Paderborn, Preußen Münster, VfL Osnabrück, 1 FC Magdeburg.

Leipzig

You can fly there from Birmingham, Edinburgh, Glasgow, Heathrow, Manchester, Newcastle.

You can easily get to RB Leipzig, Energie Cottbus, Erzgebirge Aue, Dynamo Dresden, Chemnitzer FC, Rot Weiß Erfurt, Hallescher FC, FSV Zwickau.

Munich

You can fly there from Birmingham, Bristol, Cardiff, Edinburgh, Glasgow, Heathrow, Gatwick, Luton Manchester, Newcastle, Stansted.

You can easily get to FC Bayern München, FC Augsburg, FC Nürnberg, FC Ingolstadt 04, SpVgg Greuther Fürth, SSV

Jahn Regensburg, SpVgg Unterhaching, TSV 1860 München.

Stuttgart

You can fly there from Aberdeen, Belfast, Birmingham, Edinburgh, Leeds, Gatwick, Heathrow, Manchester, Newcastle, Stansted.

You can easily get to VfB Stuttgart, TSG Hoffenheim, SC Freiburg, Heidenheim, SV Sandhausen, Karlsruher SC, VfR Aalen, SG Sonnenhof Grossaspach, Stuttgarter Kickers.

* * *

Choosing clubs and games

The best place to find out about fixtures is the **Bundesliga** website (https://www.bundesliga.com/en/). If you are interested in lower league clubs, the football magazine **Kicker** (http://www.kicker.de/)is an excellent starting point. At the top of the homepage, there are links to "Bundesliga", "2. Liga" and "3. Liga". Click on one of them and then choose "Spieltag/Tabelle" (Matchday/Table). Then you can see what's on.

Kicker also has fixtures for the five regional leagues. Choose "Regionalliga" and then the league you are interested in.

Another great way to find out about fixtures is the **Futbology App** which runs on iOS and Android. As well as providing information on clubs and leagues it will tell you in real time what games are available near to where you are.

* * *

'Matchday' means 'match weekend'

You do need to be careful when looking at fixtures lists.

The football calendar is organised around 'matchdays'. They set out well in advance which teams are playing on each 'matchday'.

However, games in the same 'matchday' slot can take place on Friday, Saturday, Sunday or even Monday. Unfortunately for the long-distance visitor, this is often only decided a few weeks ahead of the game. And of course, the nearer you get to the date in question, the harder it is going to be to get tickets and the more expensive your journey is likely to be.

My advice would be that if at all possible you should plan to arrive on a Thursday evening or Friday morning and leave on a Monday. That will give you time to take in at least three games as well as do a bit of sight-seeing.

If your heart is set on seeing one of the big names, order your ticket before you know the exact date.

Look out for English weeks

You don't get as many mid-week fixtures in Germany as you do in the UK. And when they do the German's call it an **'englische Woche'** - an English week. If you time your travel right you can use these weeks to double the number of games you see.

* * *

Getting a ticket

You can pay on the day at the smaller clubs.

It's probably best to order in advance for the larger outfits. The easiest way to do this is to call the club. All the larger teams will have someone who can speak English.

If you are feeling more adventurous, they all have online shops. Although the instructions are in German, the process is very straightforward. Ordering this way means you can choose exactly where to sit, and most clubs have a Print@Home facility which lets you print your ticket before you set off.

Your ticket usually entitles you to free travel on public transport to and from the game.

If you decide to buy when you arrive, you can often get tickets at tourist information offices, and clubs publish lists of other outlets (**Vorverkaufsstellen**) on their websites.

You will find contact details for all the clubs of the top three divisions in Chapter 3.

* * *

Should I stand or sit?

There is at least one standing section in all German football grounds. Standing tickets are much cheaper, and you will find yourself amongst the loudest, most passionate fans. You should be aware, however, that they can be tough to get hold of in bigger clubs. It is much easier to get a standing ticket at

2. Bundesliga and 3. Liga clubs. So my advice would be to pay a bit more and choose a seated section for Bundesliga games. And if you want the standing experience, go to a couple of lower league games.

2

GETTING THERE

Travel in Germany is a joy. Trains are quick, reliable and comfortable. Public transport in towns and cities is integrated so that you can use the same ticket on train, tram, bus or underground. Also, if you get the right special offer, you can travel long distances relatively cheaply.

Types of train

Long distance

InterCity Express (ICE) are Germany's fastest trains. They can travel at up to 186 mph and are ideal for long-distance travel. They are very comfortable and have superb facilities.

With speeds of up to 125 mph **InterCity (IC)** trains also cover long distances quickly. **EuroCity (EC)** trains cross into neighbouring countries (for example, Holland, France). You will have a smooth and comfortable journey on all of these trains. Most have a restaurant car, and some of the newest IC trains are double deckers.

Regional

Interregio-Express (IRE) trains connect regions.

Regional-Express (RE) and **Regional Bahn (RB)** trains are ideal for travelling across a particular region or between neighbouring towns. Some of these trains are double-deckers.

Local

You will find **S-Bahn** trains in most large cities. They cover short distances within cities or between neighbouring towns.

Many German cities have underground (**U-Bahn**) and tram (**Straßenbahn**) networks.

Saving money

Train travel in Germany needn't cost the earth, but you do need to look out for special tickets and reductions.

The cheapest way to travel long distances is to buy saver tickets (**Sparpreis** or **Supersparpreis**).

If you plan to do a lot of travelling, you can save even more money with a **BahnCard**. This costs 54.60 euros but entitles you to a 25% reduction on all fares for a year. If you are under 27, it only costs 34.20 euros.

A "**Quer-durchs-Land-Ticket**" lets you travel anywhere in Germany for a day. You have to leave after 9 am on weekdays, and you can't use it on ICE, EC, or ICE trains. However, you can travel on all regional trains. It's ideal for group travel. The first person pays 42 euros, but up to four additional travellers can join the group ticket for 6.50 euros more each. So a group of 5 can travel right across the country for just 13.60 euros each.

Länder-Tickets allow you to travel anywhere within a particular state for a day. From Monday to Friday, you have to leave after 9 am, and you can't use it on ICE, EC and IC trains. However, you can travel on any regional train and in most states use local public transport as well. These tickets have different prices, depending on the state.

Long distance buses

Of course, if you are not in a hurry, bus travel is an even cheaper way to get around.

Deutsche Bahn offers intercity bus travel to and between many major German cities.

Flixbus also provides low-cost bus travel to and right across Germany.

Local travel

Local travel arrangements are different depending on the city and region you are in. However, they all offer day and group tickets and other money-saving deals. They all have helpful websites – often with an English section – which include journey planning tools as well as fare information. You will find links to local transport organisations in the next chapter.

Look out for free matchday travel

At many clubs, your ticket includes free travel by local public transport(except ICE trains) to and from the game. This is worth investigating if you buy your ticket in advance.

Clubs based at the edge of town often provide free shuttle buses to carry fans to and from the game.

Other helpful travel websites

My favourite travel website is **The Man in Seat 61**. Its author, Mark Smith, knows everything there is to know about train travel in Europe and beyond. If you go to the Germany section you will find advice on buying tickets, interactive maps to help you plan routes, general information about travel in Germany and links to other helpful sites.

https://www.seat61.com/index.html

The English section of the **Deutsche Bahn** (German Railway) website is clear and helpful. You can plan trips and buy Print@Home and e-tickets here. They also give information and advice on the best deals.

https://www.bahn.com/en/view/index.shtml

Rail Europe is an online company that specialises in train travel. You can use them to buy tickets to and from anywhere in Europe. You provide departure, destination, date and time, and they do the rest in seconds. They will even help you with accommodation if you want.

https://www.raileurope.com/en

3

THE TOP THREE DIVISIONS AT A GLANCE

You can use the information in this chapter to decide where to go, to organise tickets and to plan your journey.

Die Bundesliga

FC Augsburg

http://fcaugsburg.de/wns/?lang=en

Email: info@fcaugsburg.de

Telephone: +49 (0) 821 455 477 0

Tickets:

https://www.lms-ticket.de/fcaugsburg/ajax.aspx?sub=Home

Nearest airports: Memmingen, Munich, Stuttgart

Local transport:

https://www.avv-augsburg.de/fahrplan/fahrplanauskunft

Ground: WWK Arena

Capacity: 28,623

Average attendance 18/19: 28,238

Address:

Bürgermeister-Ulrich-Straße 90, 86199 Augsburg

Colours: Red green white

Nickname: die Fuggerstädter (after a famous local family)

* * *

Hertha Berlin

http://www.herthabsc.de/en/

Telephone: +49(0) 1806 515301

Tickets:

http://www.herthabsc.de/en/tickets/matchday-tickets/matchday-tickets/page/25-1265-17--0.html#.Wdy5SBNSzmI

Nearest airports: Berlin Tegel, Berlin Schönefeld

Local transport: http://www.vbb.de/en/index.html

Ground: Olympiastadion

Capacity: 74,400

Average attendance 18/19: 9,259

Address: Olympischer Platz 3, 14053 Berlin

Colours: Blue white

Nickname: die alte Dame (the old lady)

***

1 FC Union Berlin

http://www.fc-union-berlin.de/start/

Email: verein@fc-union-berlin.de

Telephone: +49(0) 30656688

Tickets:

https://www.fc-union-berlin.de/tickets/ticket-office/

Nearest airport: Berlin

Local transport: http://www.vbb.de/en/index.html

Ground: An der Alten Försterei

Capacity: 22,859

Average attendance 18/19: 21,200

Address: An der Wuhlheide 263, 12555 Berlin

Colours: Red white

Nickname: Die Eisernen (the iron ones)

***

DSC Arminia Bielefeld

http://www.arminia-bielefeld.de/

Email: info@arminia-bielefeld.de

Telephone +49 (0)1806 – 51 53 02

Tickets:

https://www.eventimsports.de/ols/arminia/

Nearest airports: Dortmund, Düsseldorf, Hannover

Local transport: http://www.mobiel.de/startseite/

Ground: SchucoArena

Capacity: 26,515

Average attendance 18/19: 19,127

Address: Melanchtonstraße, 33615 Bielefeld

Colours: White and blue

Nickname: Die Blauen (the blues)

* * *

SV Werder Bremen

https://www.werder.de/en/

Email: tickets@werder.de

Telephone: +49(0) 421 434590

Tickets: https://www.werder.de/tickets/heimspiele/

Nearest airports: Bremen, Hamburg

Local transport: https://en.vbn.de/

Ground: Weser-Stadion

Capacity: 42,100

Average attendance 18/19: 41,414

Address: Franz-Böhmert-Straße 7, 28205 Bremen

Colours: Green white

Nickname: die Grün-Weißen (the green-whites)

* * *

Borussia Dortmund

http://www.bvb.de/

Telephone: +49 (0) 1806 51 5304

Tickets: https://www.eventimsports.de/ols/bvb/

Nearest airport: Dortmund, Düsseldorf

Local transport: http://www.vrr.de/en/index.html

Ground: Signal Iduna Park

Capacity: 81,359

Average attendance 18/19: 80,820

Address: Sportweg, 44139 Dortmund

Colours: Black yellow

Nickname: BVB

* * *

Eintracht Frankfurt

http://www.eintracht.de/en/news/

Email: info@eintrachtfrankfurt.de

Telephone: +49(0) 800 743 1899

Tickets: http://www.eintracht.de/en/tickets/

Nearest airport: Frankfurt

Local transport:

https://www.rmv.de/en/

https://www.vrn.de/mng/#/XSLT_TRIP_REQUEST2@init

Ground: Commerzbank-Arena

Capacity: 49,765

Average attendance 18/19: 49,159

Address:

Mörfelder Landstraße 362, 60528 Frankfurt am Main

Colours: Red black white

Nickname: die Adler (the eagles)

* * *

SC Freiburg

https://www.scfreiburg.com/

Email: karten@scfreiburg.com

Telephone: +49(0) 7613851777

Tickets: https://heimspiele-scfreiburg.reservix.de/

Nearest airports: Basel/Mulhouse/Freiburg, Stuttgart

Local transport:

http://www.rvf.de/en/fahrkarten-tarife/travelling-with-rvf/

Ground: Schwarzwald-Stadion

Capacity:

Average attendance 18/19: 23,894

Address: Schwarzwaldstraße 193, 79117 Freiburg

Colours: Red white

Nickname: Breisgau-Brasilianer (Brazilians of Breisgau)

* * *

TSG 1899 Hoffenheim

http://www.achtzehn99.de/

Telephone: +49(0) 7261 9493 0

Tickets:

https://tickets.1899-hoffenheim.de/online/index.php3?shopid=104

Nearest airport: Stuttgart

Local transport:

https://www.vrn.de/mng/#/XSLT_TRIP_REQUEST2@init

https://www.h3nv.de/

Ground: Wirsol Rhein-Neckar-Arena

Capacity: 30,150

Average attendance 18/19: 28,456

Address: Dietmar-Hopp-Straße 1, 74889 Sinnsheim

Colours: Blue white

* * *

1. FC Köln

https://fc.de/fc-info/home/?L=2

Telephone: +49 (0) 221/260 11 221

Tickets: https://www.eventimsports.de/ols/fckoeln/de/bl/channel/shop/

Nearest airports: Cologne/Bonn, Düsseldorf

Local transport:

https://www.vrsinfo.de/englisch/the-vrs/vrs-about-us.html

Ground: Rhein-Energie Stadion

Capacity: 50,997

Average attendance 18/19: 49,547

Address: Aachener Straße 99, 50933 Köln

Colours: Red white

Nickname: Die Geißböcke (the billy goats)

* * *

RB Leipzig

https://www.dierotenbullen.com/en

Email: ticketing.rbleipzig@redbulls.com

Telephone: +49(0) 341 124797 444

Tickets:

https://tickets.dierotenbullen.com/online/index.php?wes=empty_session_111&language=1&shopid=111&nextstate=2

Nearest airport: Leipzig

Local transport:

https://www.mdv.de/service/info-international/english/

Ground: Red Bull Arena

Capacity: 44,279

Average attendance 18/19: 38,380

Address: Am Sportforum 1, 04105 Leipzig

Colours: Red white

Nickname: die roten Bullen (the red bulls)

* * *

Bayer 04 Leverkusen

https://www.bayer04.de/en-us/

Email: info@bayer04.de

Telephone: +49(0) 214 5000 1904

Tickets: https://ticketshop.bayer04.de/SpielAuswahl

Nearest airports: Cologne/Bonn, Düsseldorf Dortmund

Local transport:

http://www.vrr.de/en/index.html

http://www.vrr.de/en/index.html

Ground: BayArena

Capacity: 30,210

Average attendance 18/19: 27,990

Address: Bismarkstraße 122, 51373 Leverkusen

Colours: Red black

Nickname: die Werkself (works eleven – because of links to local pharmaceutical firm Bayer)

* * *

1. FSV Mainz 05

https://www.mainz05.de/en/

Telephone: +49(0) 6131 37 550 0

Tickets:

https://www.eventimsports.de/ols/mainz05/en/heimspiele/channel/shop/index

Nearest airport: Frankfurt

Local transport: https://www.rmv.de/en/

Ground: Opel Arena

Capacity: 26,246

Average attendance 18/19: 28,766

Address: Egen-Salomon-Straße 1, 55128 Mainz

Colours: Red white

Nickname: Die Nullfünfer (the 0-Fives)

* * *

Borussia Mönchengladbach

https://www.borussia.de/english/home.html

Email: info@borussia.de

Telephone: +49(0) 1805 181900

Tickets: https://www.borussia-ticketing.de/default.aspx

Nearest airports: Düsseldorf, Cologne/Bonn, Dortmund

Local transport: http://www.vrr.de/en/index.html

Ground: Borussia-Park

Capacity: 54,067

Average attendance 18/19: 49,668

Address:

Hennes-Weisweiler-Allee 1, 41179 Mönchengladbach

Colours: Green white black

Nickname: die Fohlen (the foals)

* * *

FC Bayern München

https://fcbayern.com/en

Email: tickets@fcbayern.com

Telephone: +49 (0) 89 699 31 333

Tickets: https://fcbayern.com/en/tickets

Nearest airport: Munich

Local transport: https://www.mvv-muenchen.de/en/index.html

Ground: Allianz Arena

Capacity: 75,000

Average attendance 18/19: 75,000

Address: Werner-Heisenberg-Allee 25, 80939 München

Colours: Red white

Nickname: der FCB, die Bayern (Bavarians)

* * *

FC Schalke 04

http://www.schalke04.de/en/

Email: kundenservice@schalke04.de

Telephone: +49 (0) 180 622 1904

Tickets:

https://store.schalke04.de/tickets/schalke-04-spiele/heimspiele/

Nearest airports: Dortmund, Düsseldorf, Cologne/Bonn

Local transport: http://www.vrr.de/en/index.html

Ground: Veltins-Arena

Capacity: 62,271

Average attendance 18/19: 60,941

Address: Arenaring 1, 45891 Gelsenkirchen

Colours: Blue white

Nickname: die Königsblauen (the royal blues), die Knappen (the miners)

* * *

VfB Stuttgart

http://www.vfb.de/en/

Telephone: +49 (0) 1806 99 1893

Tickets:

https://shop.vfb.de/tickets/heimspiele/tageskarten/

Nearest airports: Stuttgart

Local transport: http://en.vvs.de/home/

Ground: Mercedes-Benz Arena

Capacity: 60,449

Average attendance 18/19: 54,551

Address: Mercedesstraße 87, 70372 Stuttgart

Colours: White red

* * *

VfL Wolfsburg

https://www.vfl-wolfsburg.de/en/info.html

Email: service@vfl-wolfsburg.de

Telephone: +49(0) 53 61 8 903 903

Tickets: https://tickets.vfl-wolfsburg.de/

Nearest airport: Hannover

Local transport:

http://www.wvg.de/fahrgastinfo/fahrplaene/erweiterte-fahrplanauskunft.html

Ground: Volkswagen Arena

Capacity: 25,713

Average attendance 18/19: 24,481

Address: In den Allerwiesen 1, 38446 Wolfsburg

Colours: Green white

Nickname: Die Wölfe (the Wolves)

Die 2. Bundesliga

FC Erzgebirge Aue

http://www.fc-erzgebirge.de/startseite/

Email: info@fc-erzgebirge.de

Telephone: +49(0) 377159820

Tickets:

http://www.fc-erzgebirge.de/startseite/

Nearest airport: Leipzig

Local transport: https://www.rve.de/fahrplan/stadt/

Ground: Sparkassen-Erzgebirgsstadion

Capacity: 15,690

Average attendance 18/19: 10,286

Address: Lößnitzer Straße 95, 08280 Aue

Colours: Purple white

Nickname: Die Veilchen (violets)

* * *

VfL Bochum 1848

http://www.vfl-bochum.de/site/start_en.htm

Email: info@vfl-bochum.de

Telephone: +49 (0) 235951848

Tickets:

https://eventimsports.de/ols/vflbochum1848/

Nearest airports: Düsseldorf, Dortmund

Local transport: http://www.vrr.de/en/index.html

Ground: Vonovia Ruhrstadion

Address: Castroper Straße 145 44791 Bochum

Capacity: 29,299

Average attendance 18/19: 17,662

Colours: Blue and white

Nickname: die Unabsteigbaren (those that can't be relegated)

* * *

Eintracht Braunschweig

http://www.eintracht.com/en/start/

Email: eintracht@eintracht.com

Telephone: +49(0)531232300

Tickets:

https://www.eventimsports.de/ols/eintracht-braunschweig/

Nearest airport: Hannover

Local transport:

https://www.vrb-online.de/bus/liniennetzplan.html

Ground: Eintracht-Stadion

Capacity: 23,325

Average attendance 18/19: 18,047

Address: Hamburger Straße 210, 38112 Braunschweig

Colours: Blue yellow

Nickname: Die Löwen (the lions)

* * *

SV Darmstadt 1898

https://www.sv98.de/

Email: tickets@sv98.de

Tickets:

https://sv98.de/home/tickets/vorverkauf/online-ticketshop/

Nearest airport: Frankfurt

Local transport: https://www.rmv.de/en/

Ground: Merck-Stadion am Böllenfalltor

Capacity: 17,400

Average attendance 18/19: 13,367

Address: Nieder-Ramstädter Straße 64285 Darmstadt

Colours: Blue white

Nickname: die Lilien (the lilies)

* * *

Fortuna Düsseldorf 1895

http://www.f95.de/home/

Email: service@f95.de

Telephone: +49(0)211 238010

Tickets:

https://tickets.f95.de/f95

Nearest airport: Düsseldorf, Dortmund, Cologne

Local transport: http://www.vrr.de/en/index.html

Ground: ESPRIT Arena

Capacity: 54,600

Average attendance 18/19: 43,857

Address: Arena-Straße 1, 40474 Düsseldorf

Colours: Red white

Nickname: Die Flingeraner (Flinger is a district of Düsseldorf)

* * *

SpVgg Greuther Fürth

https://www.greuther-fuerth.de/

Email: info@greuther-fuerth.de

Telephone: +49(0) 9119767680

Tickets:

https://www.eventimsports.de/ols/greuther-fuerth/de/auswaertskarten/channel/shop/index/redirect

Nearest airports: Nürnberg, Munich

Local transport: https://www.vgn.de/en

Ground: Sportpark Bonhof Thomas Sommer

Capacity: 18,000

Average attendance 18/19: 9,977

Address: Laubenweg 60, 90765 Fürth

Colours: White green

Nickname: Die Kleeblätter (shamrocks, cloverleaves)

* * *

Hamburger SV

https://www.hsv.de/en/overview/

Email: info@hsv.de

Telephone: +49(0) 40 4155 1887 (1 or 3)

Tickets: https://shop.hsv.de/deutsch/tickets/heimspiele/

Nearest airport: Hamburg

Local transport: http://www.hvv.de/en/index.php

Ground: Volksparkstadion

Capacity: 57,000

Average attendance 18/19: 58,865

Address: Sylvesterallee 7, 20525 Hamburg

Colours: Blue white black

Nickname: die Rothosen (the red shorts)

* * *

Hannover 96

https://www.hannover96.de/en/homepage.html

Email info@hannover96.de

Telephone: +49(0) 511 96900 96

Tickets:

https://ticketing27.cld.ondemand.com/online/index.php3?shopid=104&wes=empty_session_104&language=1&nextstate=2

Nearest airport: Hannover

Local transport:

https://www.gvh.de/linien-fahrplaene/fahrtauskunft/?L=1

Ground: HDI Arena

Capacity: 49,000

Average attendance 18/19: 38,365

Address: Robert-Enke-Straße 3, 30169 Hannover

Colours: Black white green

Nickname: die Roten (the reds)

* * *

1 FC Heidenheim 1846

https://www.fc-heidenheim.de/

Email: info@fc-heidenheim.de

Tickets:

https://www.eventimsports.de/ols/fcheidenheim/

Nearest airport: Stuttgart

Local transport: https://www.hvg-bus.de/

Ground: VOITH Arena

Capacity: 15,000

Average attendance 18/19: 11,332

Address: Schloßhausstraße 162, 89522 Heidenheim

Colours: Blue red white

* * *

Karlsruher SC

https://www.ksc.de/

Email: info@ksc.de

Telephone: +49(0) 7 219643450

Tickets:

https://www.eventimsports.de/ols/ksc/

Nearest airport: Frankfurt

Local transport: https://www.kvv.de/

Ground: Wildparkstadion

Capacity: 28,762

Average attendance 18/19: 13,204

Address: Adenauerring 17, 76131 Karlsruhe

Colours: Blue white

Nickname: KSC

* * *

KSV Holstein Kiel von 1900

https://holstein-kiel.de/wilkommen

Email: geschäftsstell@holstein-kiel-de

Telephone: +49(0) 1806570029

Tickets:

https://www.eventimsports.de/ols/holstein-kiel/

Nearest airport: Hamburg

Local transport: http://www.kvg-kiel.de/en/

Ground: Holstein-Stadion

Capacity: 11,386

Average attendance 18/19: 8,878

Address: Steenbeker Weg 150, 24106 Kiel

Colours: Blue white

Nickname: Die Störche (the storks)

* * *

1 FC Nürnberg

http://www.fcn.de/en/home/

Email: info@fcn.de

Telephone: +49(0)91194079100

Tickets:

http://www.fcn.de/tickets/

Nearest airports: Nürnberg, Munich

Local transport: https://www.vgn.de/en

Ground: Grundig Stadion

Capacity: 50,000

Average attendance 18/19: 40,372

Address: Max-Morlock-Platz 1, 90480 Nürnberg

Colours: Red white

Nickname: Der Club

* * *

VfL Osnabrück

http://www.vfl.de/

Email: info@vfl.de

Telephone: +49(0) 541 770870

Tickets:

https://www.lms-ticket.de/vfl-osnabrueck/ajax.aspx?sub=Home

Nearest airports: Dortmund, Bremen, Hannover

Local transport: https://www.vos.info/

Ground: Osnatel Arena

Capacity: 16,667

Average attendance 18/19: 11,907

Address: Scharnhorststraße, 49084 Osnabrück

Colours: Purple white

Nickname: Lila-Weiß (the lily whites)

* * *

SC Paderborn

http://www.scp07.de/

Email: info@scpaderborn07.de

Telephone: +49(0) 5251 8771907

Tickets:

https://www.eventimsports.de/ols/scp07/

Nearest airports: Dortmund, Hannover, Düsseldorf

Local transport: https://www.padersprinter.de/

Ground: Benteler Arena

Capacity: 15,000

Average attendance 18/19: 11,508

Address: Paderborner Straße 89, 33104 Paderborn

Colours: Black white blue

* * *

SSV Jahn Regensburg

https://www.ssv-jahn.de/home/

Email: info@ssv-jahn.de

Telephone: +49 0(0) 941 – 6983-0

Tickets:

https://www.ssv-jahnshop.de/ssv-jahn/ajax.aspx/shop/12873d63-d429-45c1-8ecb-1e3ab650b728/Tickets.html

Nearest airport: Munich

Local transport: http://www.rvv.de/football-fans

Ground: Continental Arena

Capacity: 15,224

Average attendance 18/19: 11,773

Address: Franz-Josef-Strauß-Allee 22, 93053 Regensburg

Colours: Red white

Nickname: Die Rothosen (redshorts)

* * *

SC Sandhausen 1916

https://www.svs1916.de/home.html

Email: info@svs1916.de

Telephone: +49(0) 62248279004-0

Tickets:

https://www.svs1916.de/ticketing/tickets-kaufen/heimspiele.html

Nearest airport: Stuttgart

Local transport:

https://www.vrn.de/mng/#/XSLT_TRIP_REQUEST2@init

Ground: Hardtwaldstadion

Capacity: 15,414

Average attendance 18/19: 6,994

Address: Jahnstraße 1, 69207 Sandhaufen

Colours: Black white

* * *

FC St Pauli

https://www.fcstpauli.com/en/

Email: info@fcstpauli.de

Telephone: +49(0) 40 31787451

Tickets:

https://www.fcstpauli.com/tickets/heimspiele/

Nearest airport: Hamburg

Local transport: http://www.hvv.de/en/index.php

Ground: Millerntor-Stadion

Capacity: 29,546

Average attendance 18/19: 29,503

Address: Harald-Stender-Platz, 20359 Hamburg

airport: Hamburg

Colours: Brown white

Nickname: Die Freibeuter (pirates)

* * *

Würzburger Kickers

https://www.wuerzburger-kickers.de/

Email: mail@wuezburger-kickers-de

Telephone: +49(0) 931 660898100

Tickets: https://fwk.reservix.de/events

Nearest airports: Nürnberg, Frankfurt

Local transport:

https://www.vvm-info.de/home/startseite/startseite.jsp

Ground: Flyeralarm Arena

Capacity: 10,054

Average attendance 18/19: 5,450

Address: Mittlerer Dallenbergweg 49, 97082 Würzburg

Colours: Red white

Nickname: die Rothosen (red shorts)

Die 3. Liga

SG Dynamo Dresden

https://www.dynamo-dresden.de/aktuelles.html

Email: verein@dynamo-dresden.de

Telephone: +49(0) 351 329 58 000

Tickets:

http://www.etix.com/ticket/o/467/dynamo-dresden?cobrand=dynamodresden

Nearest airports: Berlin, Leipzig, Prague

Local transport: https://www.vvo-online.de/de

Ground: DDV-Stadion

Capacity: 32066

Average attendance 18/19: 28,434

Address: Lennestraße 12, 1069 Dresden

Colours: Black yellow

* * *

MSV Duisburg

https://www.msv-duisburg.de/

Email: info@msv-duisburg.de

Telephone: +49(0) 20393100

Tickets:

https://www.eventimsports.de/ols/msv/

Nearest airports: Düsseldorf, Dortmund

Local transport: http://www.vrr.de/en/index.html

Ground: Schauinsland-Reisen-Arena

Capacity: 31,500

Average attendance 18/19: 15,385

Address: Margaretenstraße 5-7, 47055 Duisburg

Colours: Blue white

Nickname: Die Zebras

* * *

Hallescher FC

http://www.hallescherfc.de/

Email: club@hallescherfc.de

Telephone: +49(0) 345 4441293

Tickets:

https://eventimsports.de/ols/hfc/de/ek/channel/shop/index

Nearest airport: Leipzig

Local transport:

https://www.mdv.de/service/info-international/english/

Ground: Erdgas Sportpark

Capacity: 15,057

Average attendance 18/19: 7,732

Address: Kantstraße 2, 06110 Halle (Saale)

Colours: Red white

* * *

FC Ingolstadt 04

http://www.fcingolstadt.de/home/

Email: info@fcingolstadt.de

Telephone: +49(0) 841885570

Tickets:

http://www.fcingolstadt.de/tickets/online-tickets/

Nearest airport: Munich

Local transport: http://www.invg.de/

Ground: Audi Sportpark

Capacity: 15,800

Average attendance 18/19: 9,003

Address: Am Sportpark 1b, 85053 Ingolstadt

Colours: Black red white

Nickname: Die Schanzer (trenchermen)

* * *

1 FC Kaiserslautern

Website

Facebook Twitter

Email: info@fck.de

Telephone: +49(0) 631318800

Online Ticket Shop

Nearest airport: Frankfurt

Local transport: VRN

Ground: Fritz-Walter-Stadion

Capacity: 49,780

Average attendance 18/19: 21,140

Address: Fritz-Walter-Straße 1, 67663 Kaiserslautern

Colours: Red white

Nickname: Die roten Teufel (red devils)

* * *

Viktoria Köln

https://www.viktoria1904.de/

Email: info@viktoria1904.de

Telephone: +49 (0)221 - 995 79 515

Tickets: https://www.viktoria1904.de/kein-highlight-mehr-verpassen/tageskarten

Nearest airports: Köln/Bonn, Düsseldorf

Local transport: https://www.kvb.koeln/

Ground: Sportpark Höhenberg

Capacity: 6,214

Average attendance 18/19: 1349

Address: Sportpark Höhenberg, Günter-Kuxdorf-Weg 1, 51103 Köln

Colours: Red

* * *

VfB Lübeck

https://vfb-luebeck.de/fussball/

Telephone: +49(0) 76188788

Tickets: https://vfb-luebeck.de/fussball/shop/tickets/

Nearest airport: Hamburg

Local transport: https://www.sv-luebeck.de/en/

Ground: Lohmühle

Capacity: 15,292

Average attendance 18/19: 2,152

Address: Stadion Lohmühle, Bei der Lohmühle 13, 23554 Lübeck

Colours: Green white

* * *

1 FC Magdeburg

http://www.fc-magdeburg.de/

Email: info@fc-magdeburg.de

Telephone: +49(0) 391 990290

Tickets:

https://www.eventimsports.de/ols/fcm/

Nearest airport: Hannover

Local transport: http://www.mvbnet.de/fahrkarten/

Ground: MDCC-Arena

Capacity: 20,224

Average attendance 18/19: 18,231

Address: Friedrich Ebert=Straße 62, 39114 Magdeburg

Colours: Blue white

* * *

SV Waldhof Mannheim

https://www.svw07.de/home

Email: office@svwm.de

Telephone: +41(0) 621 76415-0

Tickets: https://www.svw07.de/stadion/tickets/tageskarten

Nearest airports: Frankfurt

Local transport: https://www.vrn.de/

Ground: Carl-Benz-Stadion

Capacity: 25,721

Average attendance 18/19: 6,509

Address: Alsenweg, 68305 Mannheim

Colours: Black blue

*　*　*

SV Meppen

http://www.svmeppen.de/

Email: info@svmeppen.de

Telephone: +49(0) 5931 93010

Tickets:

https://tickets-svmeppen.reservix.de/events

Nearest airports: Bremen, Dortmund

Local transport:

https://www.levelink.de/linienverkehr/fahrplaene/

Ground: Hämsch-Arena

Capacity: 13,815

Average attendance 18/19: 7,576

Address: Lathener Straße 15, 49716 Meppen

Colours: Blue white

*　*　*

FC Bayern München II

https://fcbayern.com/en

Telephone: +49 (0) 89 699 31 333

Nearest airport: Munich

Local transport: https://www.mvv-muenchen.de/en/index.html

Ground: Stadion an der Grünwalder Straße

Capacity: 15,000

Average attendance 18/19: 748

Address: Grünwalder Straße 2 - 4, 81547 München

Colours: Red

* * *

TSV 1860 München

http://www.tsv1860.de/

Email: info@tsv1860.de

Telephone: +49(0) 1805 60 1860

Tickets:

https://www.tsv1860-ticketing.de/tsv1860/

Nearest airport: Munich

Local transport: MVV

Ground: Grünwald Stadion

Capacity: 12,500

Average attendance 18/19: 14,953

Address: Grünwald Straße 2, 81547 München

Colours: White blue

Nickname: die Löwen (the lions)

* * *

Türkgücü München

https://turkgucu.de/de/Startseite.htm

Email: info@turkgucu.de

Tickets: https://ticket.turkgucu.de/

Nearest airport: Munich

Local transport: MVV

Ground: Städtisches Stadion an der Grünwalder Straße

In 20/21 the club will play home games at at Fliegeralarm Stadion, Würzburg

Capacity: 15,000

Average attendance 18/19: 461

Address: Türkgücü München Fußball GmbH, Heinrich-Wieland-Str. 100, 81735 München

Colours: White

* * *

Hansa Rostock

http://www.fc-hansa.de/

Email: info@fc-hansa.de

Telephone: +49(0) 381 4999910

Tickets:

https://www.lms-ticket.de/hansa-rostock/ajax.aspx/shop/1112364e-2159-4f90-8c29-9df0c1d5e87f/Heimtickets.html

Nearest airport: Hamburg

Local transport:

https://fahrplanauskunft.verkehrsverbund-warnow.de/bin/query.exe/dn

Ground: Ostseestadion

Capacity: 29,000

Average attendance 18/19: 13,895

Address: Kopernikusdtraße 17 c, 18057 Rostock

Colours: White blue

Nickname: Hansa

* * *

1. FC Saarbrücken

https://www.fc-saarbruecken.de/

Email: marketing@fc-saarbruecken.de

Telephone: +49(0) 681 97144-10

Tickets: https://shop.fc-saarbruecken.de/tickets/

Nearest airport: Frankfurt, Luxembourg

Local transport: https://saarvv.de/

Ground: Hermann-Neuberger-Stadion

Capacity: 8,644

Average attendance 18/19: 3,188

Address: Stadionstraße, 66333 Völklingen

Colours; blue black

KFC Uerdingen 05

https://kfc-uerdingen.de/

Email: geschaeftsstelle@kfc-online.de

Telephone: +49(0) 21 51 49 05 05

Tickets:

https://kfc-uerdingen.de/-geschaeftsstelle/

Nearest airport: Düsseldorf

Local transport: VRR

Ground: Grotenburg-Stadion

Capacity: 34,500

Average attendance 18/19: 4,130

Address: Uerdinger Straße 463a, 47800 Krefeld

Colours: Blue red

* * *

SpVgg Unterhaching

http://www.spvggunterhaching.de/

Email: infor@spvggunterhaching.de

Telephone: +49(0) 5931 93010

Tickets: https://ticketing.spvggunterhaching.de/

Nearest airport: Munich

Local transport: http://www.vvs.de/

Ground: Alpenbauer Sportpark

Capacity: 15,053

Average attendance 18/19: 3,255

Address: Am Sportpark 9, 82008 Unterhaching

Colours: Red blue

* * *

SC Verl

https://www.sportclub-verl.de/

Email: info@scverl.de

Telephone: +49(0)1806 700 733

Tickets: https://scverl.reservix.de/events

Nearest airports: Dortmund, Düsseldorf, Hannover

Local transport:

https://www.mobiel.de/fahrplaene/fahrplanauskunft/

Ground: Stadion an der Poststraße

Capacity: 5,153

In 2020/21 the club will play home games at SC Paderborn's Benteler Arena

Average attendance 18/19: 1,068

Address: Sportclub Verl von 1924 e.V., Poststraße 33415 Verl

Colours: White black

* * *

SV Wehen Wiesbaden

https://www.svwehen-wiesbaden.de/

Email: infor@svww.de

Telephone: +49(0) 611504010

Tickets:

https://svwehen1926wiesbaden-ticketshop.reservix.de/events

Nearest airports: Frankfurt, Cologne

Local transport: https://www.rmv.de/en/

Ground: BRITA Arena

Capacity: 13,000

Average attendance 18/19: 3,152

Address: Berliner Straße 9, 65189

Colours: Red black

. . .

FSV Zwickau

http://www.fsv-zwickau.de/

Email: kontakt@fsv-zwickau.de

Telephone: +49(0) 3 75 2119550

Tickets:

https://shop.qtixx.com/online/index.php3?shopid=248&nextstate=2

Nearest airports: Leipzig, Dresden

Local transport: https://www.nahverkehr-zwickau.de/

Ground: Stadion Zwickau

Capacity: 10,134

Average attendance 18/19: 5,225

Address: Stadionallee 1, 08066 Zwickau – Eckersbach

Colours: Red white

Nickname: die Schwäne (the swans)

4

GERMAN FOR THE FOOTBALL FAN

German fans are loud and enthusiastic. They make the atmosphere at Bundesliga games.

Have you ever wondered what they were talking, shouting and singing about?

Have you ever fancied joining in?

Here are some words and phrases to get you started.

Technical terms

Anstoß

kickoff

Abwehr

defence

Dribbling

dribbling

Doppelpass

one-two

Fallrückenzieher

bicycle kick

erste Halbzeit

first half

zweite Halbzeit

second half

Pressing

pressing

Konter

counterattack

schießen

shoot

die Schwalbe

dive

Sanctions and incidents

abseits

offside

Eckball

corner

Einwurf

throw in

Elfmeter

penalty

Foul

foul

Freistoß

free kick

gelbe Karte

yellow card

rote Karte

red card

Platzverweis

sending off

People and roles

Angriff

attack

Abwehr

defence

Elf

team

Fans

fans

Linienrichter

liner

Mittelfeldspieler

midfielder

Schiedsricher (Schiri)

referee

Spieler

player

Stürmer

Striker

Torwart

goalkeeper

Ultras

committed fans

Verteidiger

defender

Goals

das Traumtor

dream goal

das Wembleytor

doubtful goal

das Eigentor

own goal

Insults

Schiri du Arschloch!

The referee's an ....

Schieber!

Cheat!

Das war Mist/Scheiße!

That was ....

Was soll das denn?

What's that all about?

Du Penner!

Idiot!

Chants

Chants are often specific to the club, but here are two that you might hear at any Bundesliga stadium.

Steh auf wenn du für ... bist

Stand up if you're a ... fan

Auf gehts (team) schiess ein Tor

Let's have a goal

Take a look at the fan chants website to get the chants of particular clubs.

5
WHO GOES UP AND WHO GOES DOWN?

The German football league structure has changed many times since its creation at the beginning of the last century.

This is mainly because of the enormous historic and political events that have taken place in Germany over the last 120 years but is also due to efforts to make football more competitive, entertaining and profitable.

It does, however, make things a bit complicated for the occasional visitor

This is how it is at the moment.

Bundesliga

The current top tier in German football consists of 18 clubs who play each other twice in a season on 34 match days. The games for any given match day are spread across the weekend from Friday evening. Tickets for big games between two top teams or heated local derbies are likely to sell out before the exact day and time are confirmed. This makes planning for the occasional visitor a bit tricky.

There is a winter break between the first and second halves of the season, and there is no football from mid-December to mid-January. The two halves are called the *Hinrunde* and *Rückrunde*.

The last two teams are automatically relegated and the third to last plays two games (home and away) against the third from top of Bundesliga 2. These relegation/promotion play-offs can be really exciting for the neutral and agonising for fans. The encounter between Hamburger SV and Karlsruher SC is a great example. Trailing 1-0 in the second game and 3-2 on aggregate, Hamburg seemed destined for relegation. A last minute goal for Hamburg from a free kick took the game into extra time. With four minutes remaining Hamburg scored again to edge ahead for the first time in both games. There was to be one more twist when Karlsruhe were awarded a penalty for handball two minutes into stoppage time. Hamburg keeper René Adler saved the spot kick, and Hamburg emerged unlikely winners.

2. Bundesliga

The second tier also consists of 18 clubs who play each other twice in a season. Games for a given match day are also spread across a weekend.

As in the 1. Bundesliga, the last two teams are automatically relegated, and the third from last plays third from top of the 3. Liga home and away.

Many historic and well-known teams play in the 2 Bundesliga, and games can be just as exciting and passionate as those in the higher division. Average attendance in 2018/19 was 19,115, and six clubs had an average of over 20,000. My personal list of teams well worth a visit would include VfL Bochum, Fortuna Düsseldorf, Hamburger SV and FC St Pauli.

3. Liga

The third tier consists of 20 clubs who play each other twice.

Reserve teams from the upper two divisions can compete in this league.

The last three teams are automatically relegated to one of the regional leagues.

Average attendance in the 3 Bundesliga in 2018/19 was 8,128, but six teams had an average of over 10,000. If you go to see one of the teams chasing promotion, or to a local derby, you are still likely to experience the highly charged atmosphere of the higher divisions. For example, on 18 April 2015 over 25,000 fans saw Armenia Bielefeld come back from a goal down to beat local rivals Preußen Münster 2-1 and maintain their drive for promotion.

You can have a fantastic experience at third division grounds. Tickets are cheaper and easier to come by. You will have no problem getting a standing place. Transport to and from the grounds is quicker and much less crowded. You will also get a really friendly welcome.

Regionalligen

There are 55 semi-professional teams organised into five regional leagues:

- Regionalliga Nord
- Regionalliga Nordost
- Regionalliga West
- Regionalliga Südwest
- Regionalliga Bayern

Last season the winners of Regionalligen Nordost, West and Südwest won automatic promotion and the winners of Regionalligen Nord and Bayern competed in two playoff games.

Reserve teams from the top two divisions are allowed to compete in these leagues.

Attendance at Regionalliga games is considerably lower than in the higher tiers, but several clubs still have a strong fan base and can attract large crowds. Regionalliga West, for example, is home to former greats like Rot Weiß Essen, Alemannia Aachen and Rot Weiß Oberhausen.

Oberligen

The next tier down consists of 10 amateur leagues called **Oberliga** which feed into the regional leagues.

Level 6 and below

Below the Oberligen, the state football associations have their own leagues.

6

CUP COMPETITIONS

You don't have to limit your experience of German football to league games. You will also find plenty of atmosphere and excitement in cup competitions.

DFB-Pokal

What is it?

Deutscher Fußball-Bund (DFB) is the name of the German football association. It runs Germany's main knockout competition – the **DFB-Pokal**. This cup began in 1935 – although it was called the Tschammer-Pokal back then – and is held every year. It is the second-most coveted prize in German football. The winner qualifies for the Europa League and plays the league champions in the DFL-Supercup.

How does it work?

Sixty-four teams, including all the clubs from the top two divisions, take part. The first round involves all the clubs in the top two divisions as well as the top four in 3. Liga. They are joined by 21 regional cup winners and the runners-up from the three largest regional associations.

Because every team involved in the football league system can compete in local competitions, this format makes sure that every team has the chance of being involved in the DFB Cup. This potential prize lifts the status of regional tournaments and brings extra interest, excitement and income to smaller clubs.

Home advantage for giant-killers

The draw for the first round is made from two groups of 32. The first group includes the previous season's Bundesliga teams and the two 14 teams from the 2 Bundesliga. The bottom 14 teams from the 2 Bundesliga, the top 4 teams from the 3. Liga and the 24 amateur teams go into the second group. The first round is played at the home ground of the team from the second group.

The second round draw works in the same way. After that, all the remaining teams go into one group.

Although an amateur club has never won the cup, this system provides fantastic opportunities for surprise results and giant killing, as well as increased media attention and income for lower league clubs.

On to the final

If your club makes it to the final rounds, there is the chance of a trip to the Olympia Station in Berlin.

DFL-Supercup

The game between the winners of the Bundesliga and the DFB-Pokal at the beginning of the season is called the **DFL-Supercup.** If a club wins the league and cup the previous year, the Bundesliga runners-up take the second place.

Verbandspokale

For local flavour and to find out about smaller clubs you should watch a regional cup game (**Verbandspokal**). Rules vary from region to region, but these cups are usually open to any team from the 3. Liga and below. As well as local bragging rights, the prize for the winners is the chance to compete in the first round of next season's DFB Cup.

So, for a visitor to Germany, going to a regional cup game can be a great way to experience the atmosphere of a hotly contested local derby.

7
FINDING OUT MORE

Books

It's a case of quality rather than quantity when it comes to books about German football. There aren't that many, but the ones that are available are excellent.

If you read no other book about football in Germany, you should read **Tor! The Story of German Football**, by Uli Hesse. This well-researched book takes the reader through the history of German football, from its origins in the late 19th century to the present day.

There's a whole chapter on how German clubs got their names, and the story of football unfolds within the context of German history. Hesse describes how in the early days clubs had to fight for respectability in the face of opposition from the gymnastics movement, but how football gathered momentum and became a mass sport in the 1920s and 1930s. He outlines the horrors of the Nazi regime and war years and their impact on football and then goes on to the 'Miracle of Bern' when Germany won the World Cup. He covers the building of dominant sides in the '60s and 70's, the TV explosion of the late '80s, and then the low point of Euro 2000. The book ends with a description of the inexorable rise of German football from 2000 to become the world force it is today.

It is written in a very accessible style, and Hesse makes brilliant use of stories to bring facts to life.

Hesse has published two more books about German football. **Building the Yellow Wall** tells the story of Borussia Dortmund.

Bayern: Creating a Global Superclub narrates the rise and rise of Bayern Munich.

* * *

Raphael Honigstein speaks and writes knowledgeably, fluently and interestingly about football in German and English.

In **Das Reboot: How German Football Reinvented Itself and Conquered the World**, he charts German football's return from the wilderness of the late 1990s, culminating in the glorious victories over Brazil and Argentina in the 2014 World Cup finals.

* * *

Matchdays: The Hidden Story of the Bundesliga by Ronald Reng tells the story of the Bundesliga through the life and times of Heinz Höher. His career as a player spanned the years before and after the formation of the Bundesliga. He played for Bayer 04 Leverkusen,

Meidericher SV (later renamed MSV Duisburg), FC Twente and VfL Bochum. As a coach he worked for VfL Bochum, Schwarz Weiß Essen, MSV Duisburg, Fortuna Düsseldorf and FC Nürnberg, as well as teams in Greece and Saudi Arabia.

The reader experiences the history of the Bundesliga from the perspective of someone who lived it. This approach also enables Reng to give great insights into everyday life in modern Germany.

Höher himself is a fascinating and at times tragic figure. The many bitter disappointments in his life story leave the reader in no doubt about the cruelty of modern football and the narrow line between success and failure.

* * *

Robert Reng was a close friend of Robert Encke, the German goalkeeper who tragically took his own life in 2009. In **A Life Too Short: The Tragedy of Robert Enke**, Reng describes his friend's life, casting light on the crushing pressures of professional sport.

* * *

OK, **The Miracle Of Bern** is a film, not a book – but it's the best film I have ever come across about German football. Set in the gloomy post-war years when Germany was still coming to terms with its terrible past and only just recovering from the disasters inflicted on the country by National Socialism, it leads up to Germany's surprising victory in the 1954 World Cup. The film is much more than an intensely emotional and touching story. It shows us what Germany was like in the immediate post-war years and what football was like before the Bundesliga.

* * *

If you want to get into the culture and tradition of one team, **Pirates, Punks & Politics: FC St. Pauli: Falling in Love with a Radical Football Club** by Nick Davidson is the book for you. Davidson describes his development from a disillusioned ex-Watford fan, through troubled times following non-league football, to his discovery of and love affair with St Pauli. He explains how he moved from interested outsider to a regular part of the fan scene. The context for this personal journey is provided by a description of the transformation of St Pauli into a unique football club, which in turn is set within the recent history of Hamburg and Germany.

The result is a fascinating insight into the culture and traditions of a cult club, and an intriguing glimpse of how football could be if the clubs were genuinely run for and by the fans, and fully embedded in the communities they serve.

* * *

Trautman's Journey: From Hitler Youth to FA Cup Legend is the biography of the famous Manchester City goalkeeper Bert Trautmann. Although Trautmann achieved fame and fortune in English football, the book provides a fascinating picture of life in Hitler's Germany and of how the Nazi regime managed to indoctrinate young people.

* * *

The Ball is Round: A Global History of Football by David Goldblatt tells the story of football across the world. It shows the origins, development and social significance of German football in a European and global context.

* * *

The People's Game by Alan McDougal made it to the Guardian's list of best sports books of 2016. McDougal is History and European studies professor at the University of Guelph. In this book, he explains how, although the East German state managed to mould Olympic athletes in its own image, attempts by the communist dictatorship to use football for political ends failed.

* * *

Websites

The **Bundesliga** has a website in English where you can get the latest stories as well as information on fixtures and scores. It has detailed and very informative sections for each club. You can sign up for a newsletter, and there is also a dedicated **Bundesliga channel** on YouTube and a **Bundesliga App**.

- https://www.bundesliga.com/en/
- https://www.youtube.com/user/bundesliga
- https://www.bundesliga.com/en/fanzone/app/

Deutsche Welle is an international broadcaster. The English language website provides German and international news, as well as background videos and articles, links to TV programmes and German language courses. The Sports section includes reports and discussion on German football.

- http://www.dw.com/en/top-stories/s-9097

BT Sport shows top Bundesliga fixtures each week, and you can often see a 2. Bundesliga game on a Friday evening. They also have exclusive rights to the Champions League and Europa League, which feature plenty of German teams.

There are also plenty of highlights and clips.

- http://sport.bt.com/

Vavel is an international online sports paper. The German section has articles, match reports and transfer news.

- https://www.vavel.com/en/international-football/

Bleacher report is another online sports paper with plenty of current Bundesliga news and stories.

- http://bleacherreport.com/germany

The Bundesliga section of broadcaster **ESPN**'s website provides news, match reports, video clips and discussions.

- http://www.espn.co.uk/

Kicker is a very popular sports magazine. Although everything on its website is in German, you can pick up loads of information about fixtures, results and standings. It's ideal for planning a trip.

- https://www.kicker.de/

* * *

Blogs and podcasts

The **Bayer 04 Leverkusen UK Fan Club** is run by a fan and is packed with information about the club and its history as well as everything you need to know to plan a visit

- https://www.bayerleverkusenukfanclub.co.uk/

Outside Write - podcasts and articles about travel and football abroad, including plenty on Germany.

- http://outsidewrite.co.uk/category/germany/

UK Fortuna covers Fortuna Düsseldorf

- https://ukfortuna.co.uk/

Union in English - a website for Union Berlin fans.

- http://union-berlin.com/

Bayern Central - a site for Bayern Munich fans.

- https://bayerncentral.onefootball.com/

Talking Fussball - a weekly podcast from Munich.

- http://talkingfussball.com/

Fell in love with a girl - a podcast covering FC St Pauli.

- http://fellinlovewithagirlpod.libsyn.com/

The Yellow Wall - news and views about Borussia Dortmund.

- https://www.theyellowwall.net/

No prizes for guessing the subject matter of the **FC Schalke 04 Podcast**.

- https://soundcloud.com/fcschalke04podcast/

* * *

Apps and Social Media

Futbology is the perfect app for any football trip, and I can't recommend it strongly enough. It contains a database of more than 25,000 stadiums and has up-to-date fixture lists for more than 700 leagues. In the Germany section, you can find information about clubs and games right down to the 6th tier. My favourite feature is the Matches Nearby tool, which tells you which games are on near where you happen to be. You can get this brilliant app for **iOS** and **Android**.

- https://apps.apple.com/gb/app/groundhopper/id489247406
- https://play.google.com/store/apps/details?id=com.kepermat.groundhopper&hl=en_UK

European Football Weekends is a Facebook group whose members share information and stories about watching football across Europe and beyond. No matter which club you want to watch, you will find someone here with detailed local knowledge.

- https://www.facebook.com/groups/europeanfootballweekends/

Bundesliga clubs have Facebook groups and Twitter feeds in English.

MAKING THE MOST OF YOUR VISIT

Come for a long weekend

Football fixtures are played Friday evening, Saturday and Sunday afternoon and evening, and Monday evening. So if time your visit well and base yourself in the right place you could see at least three games over a long weekend. If you have chosen wisely, you will also find plenty of other things to keep you busy and entertained as well as watch football.

It all comes down to choosing the right base. It should have:

- an airport with frequent flights to major European cities.
- good train links to other parts of Germany.
- a well organised local transport system.
- at least 5 interesting football clubs within easy reach.
- lots of exciting things to do and see beyond going to games.

Others with links or a strong affinity to particular areas may disagree, but I think these are the best candidates for a long football weekend in Germany.

Berlin

Berlin is one of the most exciting cities in Europe. At every turn, you come across historic buildings and famous street names. As you would expect of the capital city of Europe's most prosperous country, it is full of shops, cafes, bars, restaurants and nightclubs.

And, of course, Berlin is the perfect base for a footballing visit to the eastern half of Germany.

Three Bundesliga clubs are within easy reach:

- Hertha Berlin
- Union Berlin
- RB Leipzig

For a 3. Liga experience try:

- 1 FC Magdeburg
- Hallescher FC

How to get there

Berlin has two international airports. **Berlin-Tegel** is to the north-west of the city and **Berlin-Schönefeld** to the south-east. You can fly to at least one of them from most major UK airports. The two airports run a combined website, which will give you a good idea of where you can fly from.

http://www.berlin-airport.de/en/index.php

Getting into town is simple:

- From Tegel, bus 128 will bring you to "Kurt-Schumacher-Platz" where you can take the U6 underground into the city centre.
- The S9 and S45 trains link Schönefeld to the wider city transport system.

You can also get to Berlin by train from most major German cities. You do need to be aware, however, that it will be a long journey from the west of the country.

Getting around

Berlin has a superb public transport system, and this is by far the best way to get around. Buses, local trains, trams and underground are all integrated into one network where you can use the same ticket.

There is an excellent section on the city website, which shows routes and explains in English how the ticketing system works.

- https://www.berlin.de/en/public-transportation/

Many visitors buy the Berlin WelcomeCard, which entitles you to free use of public transport in the city centre, reduced entrance into many tourist attractions and special offers in a range of restaurants and shops.

http://www.berlin.de/en/tourism/1895467-2975548-berlin-welcomecard.en.html

Other things to do

You could spend weeks in Berlin and still not do and see everything. Here are the places you might like to visit first if you are only here for a couple of days.

The Brandenburg Gate

This was initially conceived as an arch of peace, but it has often been used to glorify war and military power. For example, in 1933 the Nazis staged a massive torchlight procession through the gate to signify the start of their "1,000 Year Reich".

During the Cold War, the gate was right next to the Berlin Wall. It was here that US President Reagan gave his famous speech after the Wall was removed, and today it is used as a setting for events, celebrations and concerts.

Reichstag

The German parliament meets here. The building is topped by a magnificent domed roof, designed by British architect Sir Norman Foster. If you are feeling energetic, you can climb to the top and enjoy beautiful views of the city.

"Memorial to the Murdered Jews of Europe"

This monument, which is sited between the Reichstag and Potsdamer Platz, was built in remembrance of the Jews murdered by the Nazis during their reign of terror. It consists of thousands of concrete blocks.

Alexanderplatz

This used to be the centre of the former East Berlin.

Checkpoint Charlie

When the city was divided by the Berlin Wall, there were several heavily guarded crossing points between East and West. This is probably the most famous. There is a museum showing the desperate measures East Germans adopted to try and escape – and how brutally the East German regime tried to stop them.

Kurfürstendamm

The "Ku'damm" is a 2 mile long tree-lined boulevard packed with shops, restaurants and pavement cafes.

Kaiser-Wilhelm-Gedåchtniskirche

This is the ruin of a church which was hit by bombs in 1943. It has been left unrestored as a reminder of the costs of war.

Finding out more

If you have more time to spend here, or if you decide the come back for a more extended visit, you can find out more about this beautiful city in the English version of its website.

http://www.visitberlin.de/en

Düsseldorf

As you would expect of a regional capital, Düsseldorf is a vibrant and lively city offering plenty of things to do and see. And there is a huge choice of clubs to visit.

Düsseldorf is on the edge of a large metropolitan area called the **Ruhrgebiet**, which is home to some of Germany's best known and oldest football clubs. There are also plenty of clubs a bit further afield as well. There are seven Bundesliga clubs within easy reach:

- Armenia Bielefeld
- Borussia Dortmund
- FC Schalke 04
- Bayer 04 Leverkusen
- Borussia Mönchengladbach
- 1 FC Köln

There are also several 2. Bundesliga clubs nearby:

- VfL Bochum
- Fortuna Düsseldorf
- VfL Osnabrück
- SC Paderborn

These 3. Liga clubs are also easy to get to:

- MSV Duisburg
- Viktoria Köln
- KFC Uerdingen

Regionalliga West is the fourth tier of German football. These three old clubs are definitely worth a visit:

- Rot Weiß Essen
- SC Preußen Münster
- Rot Weiß Oberhausen
- SG Wattenscheid

How to get there

You can fly to Düsseldorf Rhein Ruhr Airport from Birmingham, London Stansted, London Heathrow, London Gatwick, Manchester, Cardiff, Glasgow, Newcastle.

When you come into the arrivals, follow the signs for the **S11** local train service. An escalator will take you straight from the arrivals lounge to the platform.

Buy a ticket from the red machine at the beginning of the platform – you need a single in price range A (it'll cost you 2.50 euros) – make sure its stamped – and get on the next train heading towards **Bergisch Gladbach**. The journey takes about 20 minutes, and you get off at **Düsseldorf Hauptbahnhof** (the central station).

If you're not keen on flying, Eurostar can get you there from London – with one change in Brussels – in about 5 hours.

Getting around

Local transport is safe, clean, reliable, quick, cheap and very easy to use. It's also completely integrated so you can use the same ticket on bus, tram, underground and local trains.

You have to buy tickets before you start your journey, but there are machines everywhere. Alternatively, you can get them at tourist information offices.

You can buy single tickets or a ticket that gives you four single journeys – but if you are going to be making several trips on one day the simplest solution is to get is a day ticket.

How much you pay depends on how far you want to travel.

For 6.50 euros you can get a day ticket which lets you travel anywhere you want within Düsseldorf, as many times as you want, on any means of transport all day long.

If you want to go further afield, you pay more depending on where you want to go.

If there are more than one of you, get a group day ticket, which works out even cheaper – so long as you travel together all day.

You need to make sure you stamp your ticket with the time and date you started your journey. Some tickets come ready-stamped – it will say on them "Ticket bereits entwertet". If it doesn't, all you need to do is put it into the machine which you will see on buses and trams and on the way to underground and train platforms.

If you need more information, the VRR website has a brilliant section in English which explains how fares and tickets work. They also have a really helpful journey planner.

http://www.vrr.de/en/fares-and-tickets/

Other things to do

Altstadt.

They say it's the longest bar in the world, with over 260 pubs, cafes and restaurants to suit all tastes and budgets. Many have TV screens inside and out and show games on matchdays.

Uerige

Spend some time in Uerige in Rheinstrasse. This is a famous pub which brews its own beer called Alt. They also serve traditional Düsseldorf food. You can sit down inside if you want – but there is usually a big crowd of people outside as well. You can get your drinks from a bar in the street or from waiters who come round with regular refills. While you are there, go round the corner. You will see people buying drinks from a little window beside a shop. They are buying Killepitsch – a local liqueur, which is said to be good for the digestion.

Kaiserswerth.

Take the underground (U79) to this quiet town about 15 minutes from the city centre. You can take a walk along the Rhine, have coffee and cakes (Café Schuster opposite the platform, Backerei Norgel on your left in the market place), have a typical pub meal and a beer (Bierhaus zum Einhorn in the market place) or wander around. There is a snack bar called Berliner Imbiss on the tram platform which is said to do the best Bratwurst in Düsseldorf. There are also regular boats between the city centre and Kaiserswerth, so you might want to go back on the river. If you go back by underground, get out at Heinrich Heine Allee and take a walk through the Altstadt.

Oberkassel,

The underground (U74, U77, U75 or U76) will take to Oberkassel on the other side of the river. Then walk back over the bridge, so you see the city panorama. Once you are on the other side, keep walking towards the city centre. There is a row of bar/restaurants right on the riverside – you can get a decent meal there, or you might just want to take a look at what how Germans like to unwind and have a good time.

Mediahafen.

This used to be the docks area, but all the old warehouses have either been converted into modern flats and offices or replaced by amazing new buildings.

Frankfurt

Frankfurt is Europe's biggest financial base and one of Germany's wealthiest cities. It also happens to have one of Europe's biggest and best-connected airports. Travelling to and across Frankfurt is very straightforward - and it's in the middle of beautiful countryside. Interesting Bundesliga destinations are:

- Eintracht Frankfurt
- 1 FSV Mainz 05

From the 2. Bundesliga you can choose from:

- SV Darmstadt
- 1 FC Heidenheim
- SV Wehen Wiesbaden

There are two 3. Liga clubs within range:

- 1 FC Kaiserslautern
- Würzburger Kickers

How to get there

Frankfurt airport is the fifth largest in Germany and one of the busiest in Europe. You can fly here from most major European cities as well as from Aberdeen, Birmingham, Bristol, Edinburgh, Glasgow, Heathrow, Manchester and Newcastle.

The airport has a station with frequent trains into the city centre. Just follow the signs for Airport City Mall/Regionalbahnhof.

Frankfurt station is a major hub with excellent links to cities right across Germany and Europe.

Getting around

The integrated public transport system is coordinated by RMV. They offer a special card - the RheinMainCard. For 22 euros you get free and unlimited use of all public transport in the region for two consecutive days.

> https://www.frankfurt-rhein-main.de/en/Information-Planning/RheinMainCard)

Other things to do

Alstadt

They have recently finished renovating and reconstructing the old part of town, and it's a great place to spend a free afternoon. You can now wander past carefully restored historic buildings, window shop outside small independent shops, or have a drink or a meal at one of the many cafes and restaurants.

Ebbelwei

Also called Schoppe or Stöffche, this apple wine is Frankfurt's most popular drink. They serve it in unique jugs at apple wine pubs.

Main Tower

This tower was completed in 2000. There is a viewing platform at 200 meters from where you can see the entire city and its surroundings.

Hamburg

Easy to get to and with a flourishing football culture, Hamburg is the perfect base for a visit to the north of Germany.

As you would expect of Germany's largest port, it is a relatively wealthy city with plenty to see and do as well as watch football.

Many visitors will have heard of the "Reeperbahn'. Once a notorious red-light district, this part of town is now famous for its clubs, music, theatres and bars. You will also want to visit the harbour area, maybe take a boat trip around the Alster Lake or spend some time in Hamburg's famous fish market.

And, of course, there are two famous football clubs: Hamburger SV and FC St Pauli. Both currently play in the 2 Bundesliga. The nearest Bundesliga team is Werder Bremen.

Holstein Kiel is the closest 2 Bundesliga club.

For a great 3. Liga experience you can travel to Hansa Rostock or recently promoted VfB Lübeck.

How to get there

There are cheap, direct flights to Hamburg from many UK airports, including:

Bristol, Birmingham, Edinburgh, Manchester, London Heathrow and Gatwick.

There are trains every ten minutes from the airport station into town. The journey takes 25 minutes.

Getting around

The easiest way to get around Hamburg is by public transport. Local trains, underground, buses and ferries are all integrated, and the cheapest way to travel is to buy a day ticket.

You can get more information at the main public transport website about how public transport works and what kind of ticket you should buy.

http://www.hvv.de/en/tickets/single-day-tickets/overview/index.php

The Hamburg CARD

You can buy this tourist card for one, two or three days. It entitles you to free travel on public transport, reduced entrance to many attractions and museums and discounts at selected restaurants and shops.

You can book a card ahead of your visit.

https://www.hamburg-travel.com/search-book/hamburg-card/book-online-now/

Other things to do

Maritime Museum

You can find out about Hamburg's seafaring past in this private museum, which is housed in a refurbished warehouse.

Fischmarkt

Every Sunday from 5 to 10 am there is a fish market in a district called St Pauli, where you will see all kinds of fish for sale. Next door, you can hear live music from local bands.

The Harbour

You can book boat tours of the harbour, the Alster and the many canals around them.

For more information go to

http://www.hamburg-travel.com/experience/events/alster-boat-trips/

Altstadt

Hamburg's old town was destroyed during the war but has been carefully restored. There is no shortage of cafes, shops, bars and restaurants. If you have time, you can book a guided walking tour of the city centre.

Hannover

Hannover 96, currently in the 2 Bundesliga, is the biggest club in this lovely city. And there are plenty of clubs nearby.

The Bundesliga teams you can travel to are:

- Armenia Bielefeld
- VfL Wolfsburg

2. Bundesliga clubs include:

- Eintracht Braunschweig

- VfL Osnabrück
- SC Paderborn

For a 3. Liga you can visit:

- SC Verl

How to get there

You can fly to Hannover from Birmingham, Manchester, London Heathrow and London City airports. Trains to the city centre leave every 30 minutes from the S-Bahn station in Terminal C.

You could also fly to Düsseldorf or Hamburg and continue your journey by train.

Getting around

The Hannover public transport organisation (GVH) coordinates a network of buses, trams and trains across the city and the wider area. The English section on its website provides all the information you might need about tickets, routes and times.

https://www.gvh.de/en/linien-fahrplaene/fahrtauskunft/

For information about how to reach nearby towns use the Deutsche Bahn website

https://www.bahn.com/en/view/index.shtml

Other things to do

Herrenhausen Gardens

This 300-year-old garden complex is one of Hannover's major attractions. The centrepiece, called the "Great Garden", is the best known baroque garden in Europe and tourists flock here in their thousands.

Altstadt

Hannover's old town, which was almost destroyed during the second world war, has been painstakingly restored and is now perfect if you want to do a bit of shopping, sit in a cafe or wander through the atmospheric streets.

New Town Hall

Take this curved lift to the top. As you go up, you can look through the floor at the city below. When you get to the top, you get a superb view of Hannover and its surroundings.

Leipzig

If you don't mind a bit of train travel, Leipzig is an excellent base from which to explore football in the eastern side of Germany. Since reunification, the city has established itself as a rival to Berlin as a trendy place to live and work.

The nearest Bundesliga destinations are:

- RB Leipzig
- Hertha Berlin
- Union Berlin

For a 2. Bundesliga experience you can go to:

- Erzgebirge Aue

Nearby 3. Liga clubs include:

- Dynamo Dresden
- Hallescher FC
- FSV Zwickau

The other Leipzig team, 1 FC Lokomotive Leipzig, plays in the fourth tier Regionalliga Nordost.

How to get there

There are flights to Leipzig/Halle Airport from Birmingham, Edinburgh, Glasgow, Heathrow, Manchester and Newcastle. You can then take a local train (S5) into the city centre.

There are also direct intercity train links to German cities, including Berlin, Hamburg and Munich.

Getting around

You can buy a Leipzig Card at the Tourist Information Office.

http://www.leipzig.travel/en/LEIPZIG_CARD_2054.html

It costs 11.90 euros for one day and 23.50 euros for three days and entitles you to free travel on trams, buses and local trains as well as reduced entrance to many attractions.

Other things to do

There's plenty of history in Leipzig, but it is also a very modern and vibrant place. You will have no trouble finding things to do before and after the football. Here are five suggestions:

Altstadt

The old centre of Leipzig is full of carefully restored historic buildings

Stasi Museum

The Stasi was East Germany's notorious security police force. This museum, which is based in its former Leipzig headquarters, documents how it was used to spy on the entire population and to crush any dissent.

Nikolaikirche

Events at this church contributed significantly to the peaceful overthrow of the East German regime and the eventual reunification of the country. In September 1989 huge numbers people started to gather here to pray for peace. Prayers were then followed by mass demonstrations as people marched through the streets demanding change. The largest gathering consisted of 70,000 people. Although soldiers and security police were on standby to crush these protests, the orders never came, and eventually, the DDR leadership gave in.

Zoo

Leipzig's zoo is one of the most progressive in Germany. As well as plenty of endangered species it houses 17,000 tropical plants.

Countryside

Leipzig is surrounded by beautiful countryside – perfect for a picnic or some fresh air and exercise.

Munich

Famous for beer, Lederhosen and the Oktoberfest, Munich is also a great destination for the travelling football fan. Bundesliga clubs within easy reach are:

- FC Augsburg
- FC Bayern München
- Würzburger Kickers

Nearby clubs from the 2. Bundesliga include:

- SpVgg Greuther Fürth
- 1. FC Nürnberg
- SSV Jahn Regensburg

There are also four interesting 3. Liga clubs:

- FC Ingolstadt
- Türkgücü München
- 1860 Munich
- SpVgg Unterhaching

How to get there

Munich's airport – Franz Josef Strauss Airport – is a major international destination with arrivals from all over the world.

It's quite a distance from the city centre, but underground trains leave every ten minutes. Lines S1 or S8 will get you to the central station in about 40 minutes.

Getting around

Munich has buses, trams and an underground. Everything is integrated so that you can use the same ticket on each.

The city website has an extremely helpful section in English, which explains how the system works, how to plan your journey, and what kinds of tickets you can buy.

http://www.muenchen.de/int/en/traffic/public-transport.html

Other things to do

Marienplatz

This is the city's historic central square. It is home to the Town Hall and the famous Glockenspiel Tower.

The Viktualienmarkt

This used to be a farmers' market. Nowadays you can buy all kinds of fresh food and drink here. You can often purchase ingredients at this market that you won't find anywhere else in the city. It is open every day except Sunday.

English Garden

This beautiful park is perfect for walking, sitting, listening to music, taking a nap or drinking beer. In the summer months is usually packed with locals and tourists relaxing in the fresh air.

Hofbräuhaus

This former brewery is famous amongst beer drinkers across the world for its atmosphere and history. It's also a great place to try German food.

The BMW Museum

Anyone who is even remotely interested in cars or motorbikes should take a look at this museum, which tells the story of one of Germany's iconic carmakers. You will find old and current models, as well as a view what the future.

Stuttgart

Stuttgart is a beautiful city surrounded by magnificent scenery. You can see two teams without even leaving the city, and if you are prepared to travel a bit, there is a wide choice further afield:

For Bundesliga action go to:

- 1899 Hoffenheim
- SC Freiburg
- VfB Stuttgart

The 2 Bundesliga offers:

- 1 FC Heidenheim
- SV Sandhausen

Stuttgarter Kickers, the other local team, play in fourth-tier Regionalliga Südwest

How to get there

You can fly to Stuttgart from Aberdeen, Belfast, Birmingham, Edinburgh, Leeds, London Gatwick, Heathrow, Stansted, Manchester and Newcastle. It takes 27 minutes to travel by local railway (S3) from the airport into town.

Stuttgart is also straightforward to reach by rail as the city has excellent links to major cities right across Germany and the rest of Europe.

Getting around

The organisation which coordinates the fully integrated transport system is called VVS. You can get ticket information and plan trips from their website

https://en.vvs.de/home/

The StuttCard entitles you to free use of all public transport in the Stuttgart region network as well as free or reduced entrance to many places of interest. It costs between 27 and 47 euros depending on how many days you are in the city.

Other things to do

Television tower

This 217-meter high tower has been a landmark since 1956. A ticket to go to the top cost 7 euros. As well as enjoying a fantastic view of the city and its environs, you can have a meal or a snack in the restaurant.

Market hall

Packed with stalls selling all kinds of food and drink from all over the world, the Market Hall is a brilliant place to spend an hour or two. You can get an overview of the entire market from the first-floor gallery.

Schlossplatz

This huge square is the centre of city life. They put on concerts here and shows, and it's the site of the annual Stuttgart festival. In summer it's an excellent place for a picnic, or somewhere to sit and watch the world go by.

Porsche Museum

The museum uses state-of-the-art technology and 80 vehicles to tell the story of this iconic car.

Mercedes-Benz Museum

Of course, Stuttgart is also the home of Mercedes-Benz and this superb museum takes you through the 130-year history of the company and its products.

FINAL WORDS

I hope you have found this guide interesting and helpful and that you enjoyed reading it as much as I enjoyed writing it.

I would love to hear from you if you have ideas for future projects or if you have come across a great website or book about German football.

For more information
www.bundesligaandbeyond.net
johnalder@bundesligaandbeyond.net

ALSO BY JOHN ALDER

The Football Tourist's Guide to the German Ruhrgebiet

Bordered by the rivers Rhine, Ruhr and Lippe the Ruhrgebiet is one of Germany's 'hidden gems'. A vibrant, exciting and thoroughly modern metropolis, it is steeped in history and tradition. For over 100 years it has also been the beating heart of German football.

This guidebook introduces its major cities and towns, the history, culture and traditions of its people and its football clubs. There is advice on how to plan a visit and where to find out more.

Borussia Mönchengladbach: an introduction

This book sets out to share the history, tradition, triumphs and disappointments of a great club with the English-speaking world. It tells the story of Borussia from its foundation in 1900 to the present day. As well as biographies of former players and managers and famous anecdotes, there is a wealth of background information for English speakers considering a visit to Germany or wanting to follow the club from afar.

FC Schalke 04: an introduction

In 1904 a group of young miners from Gelsenkirchen got together to play football. They had very little money, no kit to wear, no ball to play with. They didn't even have a pitch to play on. This book tells the story of how the club these young men formed grew to become **FC Schalke 04**, one of the biggest, wealthiest and best-known football clubs in the world.

Bayer 04 Leverkusen: an introduction

Bayer 04 Leverkusen is another big club with a rich and proud history. Founded in 1904 by employees of a local factory it has grown to become one of the most successful clubs in Germany.

Fortuna Düsseldorf: an introduction

This short book tells the story of Fortuna Düsseldorf - one of Germany's oldest and best-known football clubs. As well as describing the history, triumphs and disappointments of this historic club it tells the life-stories of its best-known players and coaches.

The book is also packed with practical information to help football fans plan a trip to Düsseldorf and get the most out of their time in the city and its region.